Contents

Saying the sounds	4
Segmenting the sounds in blends	5
Two letters – one sound	6
Words ending **ff**, **ll**, **ss**, **zz**, **ck**	7
Adding **s**	8
Tricky words 1	9
More than one syllable	10
Two-syllable words ending with **er**	11
The 'oi' sound oi, oy	12
The 'ai' sound ai, ay, a-e	13
Adding **ing** and **er**	14
Tricky words 2	15
The long 'i' sound igh, i-e, y	16
The long 'e' sound ee, ea	17
The long 'o' sound oa, o-e, ow	18
The long 'oo' sound oo, ue, ew	19
Compound words	20
Tricky words 3	21
The 'ur' sound ur, ir, er	22
The 'ow' sound ow, ou	23
Words ending with 'v' and 'j' sounds ve, ge, dge	24
Words ending with the 'ch' sound ch, tch	25
Adding **s** or **es**	26
Tricky words 4	27
The 'or' sound or, aw, ore, oor	28
Short 'u' and short 'e' sounds oo, ea	29
Spelling words starting with **wh**	30
Spelling words starting with **kn**	31
Adding **ed**	32
Tricky words 5	33
The 'ear' sound eer, ear	34
The 'air' sound air, ear, are	35
The 'k' sound	36
Words ending with the 's' sound	37
Two-syllable words ending with long 'e'	38
Tricky words 6	39
Answers	40

Saying the sounds

Remember

Break words up into sounds. Write the letter for each sound.
dog   d-o-g

Try it

1. Write in the missing letter.

   Use **d**, **g** or **m**.   pi__   ja__   li__
   Use **b**, **z** or **j**.   __us   __ip   __ab
   Use **e**, **a** or **o**.   g__p   b__x   j__t

2. Write in the missing letters to complete the word.

   Mum and D____   Hop on one l____.
   a fishing n____   The sun is h____.
   not good: b____   Go to b____.
   not thin: f____   Five and one make s____.
   I c____ do it.    This is a ____.

Read–cover–write

Read this sentence and remember it. Then cover it and write it underneath.

Sam fed his pet cat.

_____

Check your spellings with the answers on page 40. Test yourself, or get a friend to test you.

I can break words into sounds to spell them. ☐

Segmenting the sounds in blends

Remember

When you spell words like these, listen for the two sounds in the blend.

w-e-n-t   j-u-m-p   s-p-o-t   s-w-i-m

Try it

1. Write in the missing letter. Use **n**, **s** or **l**.

   ha _ d   a _ d   a _ k
   ju _ t   e _ d   si _ k
   he _ p   fa _ t   sa _ d
   mu _ t   la _ t   fe _ t

2. Write in the missing letter. Use **t**, **r** or **l**.

   f _ om   b _ ack   p _ ant
   d _ op   s _ ill   g _ in
   s _ op   g _ an   f _ ag
   f _ op   s _ ep   s _ amp

Read–cover–write

Read this sentence and remember it. Then cover it and write it underneath.

Gran and I went to get help.

___

Check your spellings with the answers on page 40. Test yourself, or get a friend to test you.

I can segment the sounds in blends.

Spelling 1

Two letters – one sound

Remember

Some sounds need more than one letter. Say and count the sounds in these words.

dish – d-i-sh   ch-i-p   th-i-n   p-ar-t   f-or

Try it

1 Choose the letters to make the word. Write them in.

fi___	**ch sh**	mu___	**th ch**	___ink	**th sh**
ri___	**sh ch**	wi___	**sh ch**	___ip	**th sh**
wi___	**th ch**	ru___	**th sh**	fla___	**sh th**
su___	**th ch**	___op	**th ch**	___ing	**sh th**

2 Choose **or** or **ar** to make the word. Write in the missing letters.

j _ar_   c___n   ___m
c___   d___k   st___t
f___k   b___k   st___m
st___   s___t   h___d

Read–cover–write

Read this sentence and remember it. Then cover it and write it underneath.

I rush to the start.

_____

Check your spellings with the answers on page 40. Test yourself, or get a friend to test you.

I can spell words where two letters make one sound. ☐

Words ending ff, ll, ss, zz, ck

Remember

Short words ending in 'f', 'l', 's', 'z' and 'k' sounds often have these spellings.

hu**ff** fe**ll** me**ss** bu**zz** sa**ck**

Try it

1. Write in the two letters for the missing sound.

o___	**ll ff**	wi___	**ll ss**	cro___	**ff ss**
mi___	**ss ff**	te___	**ff ll**	du___	**ss ck**
ba___	**ck ff**	fi___	**zz ck**	sni___	**ff ll**

2. Write in the missing letter to spell the **ff**, **ll**, **ss**, **zz** or **ck** ending.

flo___k   stic___   fil___
nec___   kis___   mes___
puf___   bla___k   tic___
fiz___   fus___   dol___

3. Complete the word. The clue in brackets will help you.

m____(not a hit) w____(not ill) p____(not push) b____(ring it)

Read–cover–write

Read this sentence and remember it. Then cover it and write it underneath.

Jack and Jill went up the hill.

_____

Check your spellings with the answers on page 40. Test yourself, or get a friend to test you.

I can spell words ending in ff, ll, ss, zz and ck. ☐

Adding s

Remember

When there is more than one, add **s** to the end of the word.
one car   two car**s**

Try it

1 Write in the missing letters to complete the word.

Two h_____ clap.   two st_____ up the ladder

fish and ch_____   two d_____ on the pond

three jam j_____   Two pl_____ grow in pots.

lots of st_____   two fl_____

2 Write in the missing word.

one frog, two _____   one desk, two _____

one swing, two _____   one stamp, two _____

one brick, two _____   one drop, two _____

one card, two _____   one sock, two _____

Read–cover–write

Read this sentence and remember it. Then cover it and write it underneath.

He sticks six stamps on the six cards.

_____

Check your spellings with the answers on page 41. Test yourself, or get a friend to test you.

I can add s if there is more than one. ☐

Tricky words 1

Check that you can spell these words. Test yourself, or get a friend to test you.
Tick the word when you can spell it.

I ☐	to ☐	my ☐	so ☐
he ☐	you ☐	that ☐	be ☐
the ☐	was ☐	go ☐	of ☐
her ☐	no ☐	me ☐	see ☐
she ☐	we ☐	by ☐	into ☐

Read–cover–write

Read each sentence and remember it. Then cover it and write it underneath.

We went to the top of the hill.

_____

It was her car by the shops.

_____

Can you help me with my sum?

_____

I can see a jar but no jam.

_____

She will go into that shop.

_____

I will be so glad to help you.

_____

More than one syllable

Remember

A longer word can be split into parts (or syllables) to help you spell it.

sudden – sud/den   pulling – pull/ing

Try it

1. Write in the missing part of each word.

   zig z____ (criss cross)   vis i____ (go to see)

   sun s____ (dusk)   cob w____ (made by a spider)

   fin i____ (the end)   rab b____ (a pet)

   mor n____ (not night)   sand p____ (to play in)

   chil d____ (boys and girls)   se v____ (a number)

2. Add **ing** to the end of these doing words. Then use the words in the sentences.

   peck____   buzz____   bark____   bang____

   Dogs are _____.   The hens are _____.

   Bees are _____.   She is _____ the drum.

Read–cover–write

Read this sentence and remember it. Then cover it and write it underneath.

The dog is barking at the rabbit.

_____

Check your spellings with the answers on page 41. Test yourself, or get a friend to test you.

I can break up longer words to help me spell them. ☐

Two-syllable words ending with er

Remember

Say the 'er' sound clearly when you spell a word with this ending.

cor/n**er**   thun/d**er**   bet/t**er**   sum/m**er**

Try it

1. Write **er** to spell these words. Then copy the words on the line underneath.

   e v ____   ne v ____   ri v ____   af t ____   un d ____

   _____

2. Write in the second part of the word. The clue in brackets will help you.

   jum **per**   let ____ (a, b or c)
   sil ____ (not gold)   fin ____ (part of a hand)
   sis ____ (not a brother)   sup ____ (a meal)
   num ____ (1 or 2)   cle ____ (brainy)
   win ____ (after autumn)   un ____ (not over)

Read–cover–write

Read this sentence and remember it. Then cover it and write it underneath.

My sister never has supper after seven.

_____

Check your spellings with the answers on page 41. Test yourself, or get a friend to test you.

I can spell two-part words ending with **er**. ☐

Spelling 1 — Schofield & Sims

The 'oi' sound

Remember

At the end of a word the 'oi' sound is spelt **oy**.
oil   b**oy**

Try it

1. Spell these words. Write in **oi** or **oy**.

   b___l   j___n   t___   ___l   p___nt
   b___   j___   sp___l enj___ ann___
   c___n   s___l   c___l   f___l   t___l

2. Copy each word into the correct box.

'oi' sound in the middle	'oi' sound at the end

3. Complete the word with **oi** or **oy** and then add **ing**.

   b___l____   j___n____   p___nt____
   enj____ ____   ann____ ____   sp___l____

Read–cover–write

Read this sentence and remember it. Then cover it and write it underneath.

The boy will enjoy his toy car.

_____

Check your spellings with the answers on page 41. Test yourself, or get a friend to test you.

I can choose between **oi** and **oy** to spell words. ☐

The 'ai' sound

Remember

Use **ay** at the end of words.   way
Use **ai** or **a-e** in the middle of words.   made   sail

Try it

1. Spell these words. Write in **ay** or **ai**.

   d____   pl____   p____n   g____n   tr____n   st____

   r____n   m____   s____   p____nt   ag____n   aw____

2. Write the word next to the picture. Then write four words that rhyme with it.

    ____ai__   ____a__e

   f____   r____   m____   b____

   n____   t____   t____   sh____

3. Follow the pattern. Write five more words to rhyme with the first word.

   game   c_____   s_____   n_____   fl_____   sh_____

   wave   g_____   s_____   br_____   c_____   sh_____

Read–cover–write

Read this sentence and remember it. Then cover it and write it underneath.

The train came late again today.

_____

Check your spellings with the answers on page 41. Test yourself, or get a friend to test you.

I can choose between **ai** and **a-e** and **ay** to spell words. ☐

Adding ing and er

> **Remember**
>
> You can add **ing** or **er** to the end of some words. Adding the ending makes an extra syllable.
>
> p**ai**nt   p**ai**nt**ing**   p**ai**nt**er**

> **Try it**

1 Complete the **ing** words.

cross____ the road   fi_____ with a rod

tell____ a joke   ju_____ on the bed

milk____ a cow   st_____ the race

ask____ the time   thi_____ with my brain

miss____ the bus   pl_____ a game

                         sai_____ a boat

2 Add **er** to each word. Then write the new word.

hang___ _____   help___ _____

buzz___ _____   sing___ _____

stick___ _____   play___ _____

> **Read–cover–write**

Read this sentence and remember it. Then cover it and write it underneath.

I had a sticker for helping.

_____

Check your spellings with the answers on page 42. Test yourself, or get a friend to test you.

I can add **ing** and **er** to words I can spell. ☐

14

Tricky words 2

Learn to spell these words. Say the sounds and find the tricky bit. Use the empty rows for other words that you find tricky.

Read and look.	Write it. Say the sounds.	Write it. Find the tricky bit.	Remember it. Cover it. Write it.	Check. ✓
they				
there				
were				
are				
said				
have				
like				
some				
come				
look				

Read–cover–write

Read each sentence and remember it. Then cover it and write it underneath.

Some children were still there.

Come and look. There are six snails.

The long 'i' sound

Remember

Use **i-e** in the middle of words or **igh** before **t**.   time   tight
At the end of a word **y** is the most likely long 'i' spelling.   my   by

Try it

1. Write the word next to the picture. Then write four words that rhyme with it.

fl___   li____

dr___   tr___   n____   m____
sk___   cr___   r____   br____

2. Write the words in each box. Add some more words starting with **m, f, t** or **h**.

ine	ive	ike	ide	ile	ight
n___	d___	l___	s___	sm___	s___
l___	dr___	b___	sl___	___	___
___	___	___	___	___	___
___	___	___	___	___	___

Read–cover–write

Read this sentence and remember it. Then cover it and write it underneath.

The right time is five to nine.

Check your spellings with the answers on page 42. Test yourself, or get a friend to test you.

I can choose **igh, i-e** or **y** to spell words with the long 'i' sound. ☐

The long 'e' sound

Remember

The main long 'e' spellings are **ee** and **ea**.
see   tea   feet   mean

Try it

1. Follow the pattern. Write two words to rhyme with the first word.

   beach → t_____ → r_____
   team → cr_____ → dr_____
   deep → w_____ → cr_____
   keen → s_____ → b_____
   heat → b_____ → s_____
   weed → sp_____ → bl_____

2. Draw a circle round the correct spelling.

   grean   green   three   threa
   each   eech   sleep   sleap
   eet   eat   sheap   sheep
   tree   trea   these   thees

Read–cover–write

Read this sentence and remember it. Then cover it and write it underneath.

I was asleep on the beach in the heat.

_____

Check your spellings with the answers on page 42. Test yourself, or get a friend to test you.

I can choose between **ee** and **ea** to spell words. ☐

Spelling 1

The long 'o' sound

Remember

The main long 'o' spelling at the end of a word is **ow**.   low
In the middle of a word the main spelling is **o-e** or **oa**.
h**o**m**e**   c**oa**ch

Try it

1. Choose the correct spelling for these words. Write in **ow** or **oa**.

   sn____   b____st   sh____   gr____   l____f
   t____st   sl____   yell____   r____st   bl____

2. Write the words in each box. Add some more words starting with **h** or **p**.

oat	oad	oke	ose	ope	ole
b____	r____	j____	n____	sl____	st____
c____	t____	w____	r____	r____	____
g____	l____	sm____	____	____	____
fl____					

Read–cover–write

Read this sentence and remember it. Then cover it and write it underneath.

I hope we get home if it snows.

_____

Check your spellings with the answers on page 42. Test yourself, or get a friend to test you.

I can choose between **oa**, **o-e** and **ow** to spell words. ☐

The long 'oo' sound

Remember

In the middle of a word the long **oo** spelling is **oo** or sometimes **u-e**.
food   rude
At the end of a word the spelling is **ue**, **ew** or sometimes **oo**.
true   threw   boo

Try it

1. Write five words to rhyme with the first word. Make sure you use the correct spelling.

cool	p_____	f_____	t_____	st_____	r_l_
room	z_____	b_____	br_____	gl_____	d_____
root	b_____	t_____	h_____	sh_____	sc_____
noon	m_____	s_____	t_n_	sp_____	J_n_

2. Spell the words. Use **ew**, **ue** or **oo**.

 The plane fl____.

The plants gr____.   Ch____ your food.
The sky is bl____.   Stick it with gl____.
Give me a cl____.   We went to the z____.

Read–cover–write

Read this sentence and remember it. Then cover it and write it underneath.

The boy threw food across the room.

_____

Check your spellings with the answers on page 43. Test yourself, or get a friend to test you.
I can spell words with the 'oo' sound. ☐

Compound words

Remember

Split a compound word into two words. Write each little word to spell the compound word.

moonlight → moon light

Try it

1. Write in the other word to spell these compound words.

   bed r_____   play t_____   corn f_____
   farm y_____   milk sh_____   tea sp_____
   rail w_____   sun sh_____   rain c_____
   after n_____   lap t_____   book sh_____

2. Look at the picture or read the clue. Write the compound word.

   s_____ m_____    post c_____
   s_____ s_____ (at the beach)   S_____ d_____ (before Monday)
   s_____ teen (14, 15, …)   w_____ e_____ (after Friday)
   n_____ t_____ (17, 18, …)   bl_____ bell (flower)

Read–cover–write

Read this sentence and remember it. Then cover it and write it underneath.

I need my raincoat this afternoon.

_____

Check your spellings with the answers on page 43. Test yourself, or get a friend to test you.

I can split compound words into two words to spell them. ☐

Tricky words 3

Learn to spell these words. Say the sounds and find the tricky bit. Use the empty rows for other words that you find tricky.

Read and look.	Write it. Say the sounds.	Write it. Find the tricky bit.	Remember it. Cover it. Write it.	Check. ✓
little				
here				
do				
out				
most				
none				
one				
two				
three				
four				

Read–cover–write

Read each sentence and remember it. Then cover it and write it underneath.

Four little boats sail out of here.

One and two is three.

The 'ur' sound

Remember

The 'ur' sound has different spellings in different words. It can be spelt ur, ir or er.   fur   sir   her

Try it

1. Say the sounds in these words. Use a coloured pencil to write over the letters that spell the 'ur' sounds.

burn   curl   first   third   hurt
dirt   girl   skirt   shirt   church
perch   turn   surf   burst   stir
term   bird

2. Copy the words into the correct box.

ur	ir	er

Read–cover–write

Read this sentence and remember it. Then cover it and write it underneath.

The girl was first to burn the toast.

Check your spellings with the answers on page 43. Test yourself, or get a friend to test you.

I can spell words with ur, ir and er.

The 'ow' sound

Remember

Use **ow** at the end of a word.   c**ow**

Use **ow** or **ou** in the middle of words.   br**ow**n   c**ou**nt

Try it

1. Write the word next to the picture. Then write the four rhyming words with the same spelling.

 c_____    cr_____

n____   w____   t____n   cl____n
h____   P____!   d____n   fr____n

2. Follow the pattern. Write four words to rhyme with the first word.

out → sh_____   ab_____   sp_____   sc_____
sound → f_____   r_____   gr_____   p_____

3. Write in **owl**, **oud** or **outh** to make a word.

h_____   cl_____   m_____   gr_____
l_____   pr_____   pr_____   s_____

Read–cover–write

Read this sentence and remember it. Then cover it and write it underneath.

I found a brown cow going round town.

_____

Check your spellings with the answers on page 43. Test yourself, or get a friend to test you.

I can choose **ow** or **ou** to spell words. ☐

Words ending with 'v' and 'j' sounds

Remember

English words do not end with the letters **v** or **j**.
A 'v' sound at the end is spelt **ve**.
A 'j' sound at the end is spelt **ge**, or **dge** after a short vowel.

Try it

1. Spell these words ending with a 'v' sound. Write the whole word.

   giv _____   solv _____   sleev _____
   hav _____   abov _____   leav _____
   liv _____   glov _____   starv _____

2. Spell these words ending with a 'j' sound. Write the whole word.

   paje _____   larj _____   raje _____
   staje _____   caje _____   aje _____

3. These words all have a short vowel before the 'j' sound. Write in **dge** to spell the word.

   bri_____   fri_____   bu_____   ba_____
   smu_____   do_____   ju_____   nu_____

Read–cover–write

Read this sentence and remember it. Then cover it and write it underneath.

I live on a large barge by the bridge.

_____

Check your spellings with the answers on page 44. Test yourself, or get a friend to test you.

I can spell words that end with 'v' or 'j' sounds. ☐

Words ending with the 'ch' sound

Remember

At the end of a word, when 'ch' comes straight after a short vowel, it is often spelt **tch**.

i**tch**   ha**tch**

Try it

1. Write in **itch**, **atch** or **etch** to make a word.

   c_____   w_____   f_____

   sk_____   st_____   d_____

   m_____   w_____

2. Spell these words ending with a 'ch' sound.
   Use **tch** straight after a short vowel. Use **ch** in all other words.

   tea____   coa____   tor____   sna____
   hu____   pa____   chur____   per____
   bran____   ben____   lun____   mar____
   pin____   bun____   crun____   scra____
   no____   pi____   ar____   por____
   la____   stre____   mun____   bea____

Read–cover–write

Read this sentence and remember it. Then cover it and write it underneath.

Switch on the torch or fetch me a match.

_____

Check your spellings with the answers on page 44. Test yourself, or get a friend to test you.

I can choose the correct spelling for the 'ch' sound at the end of words. ☐

25

Adding s or es

Remember

If you add **s** to a word and it sounds like 'iz', it is spelt **es**.
Listen for the extra beat when **es** is added.
torch → torch**es**   dish → dish**es**

Try it

1 Complete the lists. Add **s** or **es** for more than one. Listen for 'iz' sounds that tell you to add **es**.

1 goat, 3 g_____   1 weed, 3 w_____   1 match, 3 m_____
1 team, 3 t_____   1 patch, 3 p_____   1 coach, 3 c_____
1 toy, 3 t_____   1 bench, 3 b_____   1 coin, 3 c_____
1 kiss, 3 k_____   1 night, 3 n_____   1 snail, 3 s_____
1 girl, 3 g_____   1 wish, 3 w_____   1 branch, 3 b_____

2 Finish the word that says what each thing does.

A snake hi_____.  A boat fl_____.
A teacher tea_____.   A can of pop fi_____.
A plant gr_____.   A rash it_____.

Read–cover–write

Read this sentence and remember it. Then cover it and write it underneath.

The three fishes had three wishes.

_____

Check your spellings with the answers on page 44. Test yourself, or get a friend to test you.

I can add **es** to words if I hear an 'iz' sound and an extra beat. ☐

Tricky words 4

1 Learn to spell these words. Say the sounds and find the tricky bit.

Read and look.	Write it. Say the sounds.	Write it. Find the tricky bit.	Remember it. Cover it. Write it.	Check. ✓
all				
call				
small				
old				
sold				
cold				
find				
kind				
mind				

2 Make 13 words by adding these letters to the words **old** and **all**.

t c s w h b f sm _____

_____

Read–cover–write

Read this sentence and remember it. Then cover it and write it underneath.

Find a gold coach to go to the ball.

_____

Check your spellings with the answers on page 44. Test yourself, or get a friend to test you.

I can spell all the words on this page. ☐

The 'or' sound

Remember

In the middle of words, 'or' can be spelt **aw**.   sort   dawn
At the end of words, **ore** or **aw** are most likely.   sore   jaw

Try it

1. Write in the missing letters. Use **or** or **aw**.

   A rose has th___ns.   Blow the h___n.   n___th and south
   creep and cr___l   a sleepy y___n   tall and sh___t

2. Use a coloured pencil to write over the letters that make the 'or' sound.

   saw   paw   door   floor   core   score
   draw   straw   more   before   claw   shore

3. Copy the words into the correct box. Learn the correct spellings.

ore	aw	Other spelling

Read–cover–write

Read this sentence and remember it. Then cover it and write it underneath.

I saw straw and corn on the floor.

_____

Check your spellings with the answers on page 44. Test yourself, or get a friend to test you.

I can spell words with the 'or' sound. ☐

Short 'u' and short 'e' sounds

Remember

In some words short 'u' and 'e' sounds are spelt like long vowels.
st**oo**d (oo = 'u')   br**ea**d (ea = 'e')

Try it

1. Write these words with the correct spelling.

   gud _____   fut _____
   hud _____   flud _____
   wull _____   blud _____

2. Write the correct spelling for these words.

   hed _____   def _____
   spred _____   tred _____
   ded _____   insted _____

3. Write the word next to the picture. Then write four words that rhyme with it.

   b_____

   l_____   t_____   h_____   sh_____

Read–cover–write

Read this sentence and remember it. Then cover it and write it underneath.

The cook said this bread is good to eat.

_____

Check your spellings with the answers on page 45. Test yourself, or get a friend to test you.

I can spell words where short 'e' is spelt **ea** and short 'u' is spelt **oo**. ☐

Spelling 1   Schofield & Sims

Spelling words starting with **wh**

Remember

Some words start with **wh** rather than **w**.   **wh**isk   **wh**ite

Try it

1. Read these words. Use a coloured pencil to write over the words that start with **wh** rather than **w**.

   wind   with   when   wide   while
   went   where   why   wish   which

2. Copy the words into the correct box.

w words	wh words
_____	_____
_____	_____

3. Read the clue and write the **wh** word

   Which **wh** word do cats have?   wh _____

   Which **wh** word do cars have?   wh _____

Read–cover–write

Read this sentence and remember it. Then cover it and write it underneath.

What will the wind whisper when it sees the whale?

_____

Check your spellings with the answers on page 45. Test yourself, or get a friend to test you.

I can spell some words that start with **wh**. ☐

30

Spelling words starting with kn

Remember

Sometimes a 'n' sound at the start of a word is spelt **kn** rather than **n**.

knitting

Try it

1. Draw a circle round the words with a **n** sound spelt **kn**.

   neat   knee   keep   knob   king   knew
   knife   neck   know   noon   nose   kite

2. Write the five **kn** words on the line below.

   _____

3. Write in the missing **kn** words.

   Kn_____ on the door.   Bend your kn_____.
   Cut with a kn_____.   Kn_____ me a scarf.
   Kn_____ to pray.   Tie a kn_____.
   Jack kn_____ the way.   a kn_____ in shining armour

Read–cover–write

Read this sentence and remember it. Then cover it and write it underneath.

Now I know how to knit.

_____

Check your spellings with the answers on page 45. Test yourself, or get a friend to test you.

I can spell some words that start **kn** not **n**. ☐

Adding ed

Remember

Add **ed** to action words if something has already happened.
I play football. Last week I play**ed** football.

Try it

1 Write these words with **ed** added to them.

pull _____   bark _____   wish _____
sniff _____   rush _____   fill _____
join _____   sail _____   look _____
turn _____   call _____   march _____
cross _____   toast _____   stamp _____

2 Write in the missing word.

On Monday, I mi_____ the bus.
Last week, I he_____ Dad fix the car.
After a while, the kettle b_____.

Read–cover–write

Read this sentence and remember it. Then cover it and write it underneath.

I marched up the road and turned the corner.

_____

Check your spellings with the answers on page 45. Test yourself, or get a friend to test you.

I can add **ed** to words. ☐

Tricky words 5

Learn to spell these words. Say the sounds and find the tricky bit. Use the empty rows for other words that you find tricky.

Read and look.	Write it. Say the sounds.	Write it. Find the tricky bit.	Remember it. Cover it. Write it.	Check. ✓
Mr				
Mrs				
oh				
their				
over				
your				
saw				
asked				
what				
want				

Read–cover–write

Read each sentence and remember it. Then cover it and write it underneath.

Mr and Mrs Brown have lost their dog.

_____

Oh, I saw your dog run over the bridge.

_____

The 'ear' sound

Remember

In most words, the 'ear' sound is spelt *ear*. But some words have a different spelling.   ear   cheer

Try it

1. These words all have the **ear** spelling. Read the clue. Write the word.

   You h____ with your ____s.

   a y____ (12 months)   b____d (on a hairy chin)

   cl____ (not cloudy)   D____ (you start a letter with this)

   n____ (not far)   t____s (you cry these)

2. Use a coloured pencil to write over the letters that make the 'ear' sound in these words.

   sneer   cheer   fear   here   shear
   peer   gear   beer   spear appear

3. Copy the words that do not have the **ear** spelling.

   _____

Read–cover–write

Read this sentence and remember it. Then cover it and write it underneath.

Hear the cheer when the teams appear!

_____

Check your spellings with the answers on page 45. Test yourself, or get a friend to test you.

I can spell words with the 'ear' sound. ☐

The 'air' sound

Remember

The 'air' sound can be spelt air, are or ear.   air   glare   bear
But some words have a different spelling.

Try it

1. Write the words with the same spelling as the first word.

   chair   st_____   h_____   f_____   p_____
   dare   sh_____   c_____   sc_____ st_____
   bear   p_____   w_____   sw_____

2. Each missing word has an **air** sound. Write it on the line.
   Use the correct spelling.

   Do p_____ grow on trees?   It's not here but th_____.
   Goldilocks met three b_____.   Don't st_____ at me.
   I go up the s_____ to bed.   I don't c_____.
   Brush my h_____.   I w_____ a hat in winter.
   Sit on the ch_____.   three p_____ of boots

Read–cover–write

Read this sentence and remember it. Then cover it and write it underneath.

The bear on the stair gave me a scare.

_____

Check your spellings with the answers on page 46. Test yourself, or get a friend to test you.
I can spell words with the 'air' sound. ☐

The 'k' sound

Remember

At the end of a word, a 'k' sound is spelt **ck** when it comes straight after a short vowel. It is spelt **k** in other words.

clo**ck**   sin**k**   par**k**

Try it

1 Spell these words. Write in **ck** or **k**.

ti___	pi___	ba___	dar___
thin___	mar___	bar___	for___
pa___	ban___	tra___	tru___
drin___	ro___	as___	than___

2 A 'k' sound is sometimes spelt **k** and sometimes spelt **c**.

ki → ___t → ___ck → ___d → ___ill

ski → ___d → ___p → ___n → ___ill

cr → ___ab → ___isp → ___ack → ___oss

sc → ___ar → ___arf → ___ab → ___are

Read–cover–write

Read this sentence and remember it. Then cover it and write it underneath.

Ask for a drink of milk and a packet of crisps.

_____

Check your spellings with the answers on page 46. Test yourself, or get a friend to test you.

I can spell words with **k** or **ck** for a 'k' sound. ☐

Words ending with the 's' sound

Remember

At the end of a word, use **ss** after a short vowel. **mi**ss
Use **se** or **ce** after a long vowel or another letter. **nur**se   **prin**ce

Try it

1. Spell these words. Write in **ss** or **se**.

   hou___   hi___   goo___
   mou___   chee___   cro___
   me___   hor___   cur___
   pur___   dre___   grea___
   plea___   noi___   pa___

2. These words all end with **ce**. Write words to rhyme with the first word.

   space   r_____   f_____   pl_____   tr_____
   ice   d_____   sl_____   n_____   pr_____
   chance d_____   gl_____   pr_____

Read–cover–write

Read this sentence and remember it. Then cover it and write it underneath.

Please tell the horse to make less noise.

_____

Check your spellings with the answers on page 46. Test yourself, or get a friend to test you.

I can spell words ending with **ss**, **ce** and **se**. ☐

Two-syllable words ending with long 'e'

Remember

At the end of two-syllable words, a long 'e' sound is spelt **y** or sometimes **ey**.   thirt**y**   cop**y**   troll**ey**

Try it

1. Add the second syllable to each word.

   birthday par____   The case is hea____.
   busy bo____   lime jel____
   hot and thirs____   sil____ billy
   nice and stea____   co____ cat
   Are you rea____?   I feel hap____.

2. Add the second syllable of each word. Use **key**, **ney** or **y**.

      mon____

   tur____   chim____   stor____
   fair____   don____   ho____

Read–cover–write

Read this sentence and remember it. Then cover it and write it underneath.

The jelly for the party was very heavy.

_____

Check your spellings with the answers on page 46. Test yourself, or get a friend to test you.

I can spell two-syllable words ending with a long 'ee' sound spelt **y** or **ey**. ☐

Tricky words 6

Learn to spell these words. Say the sounds and find the tricky bit. Use the empty rows for other words that you find tricky.

Read and look.	Write it. Say the sounds.	Write it. Find the tricky bit.	Remember it. Cover it. Write it.	Check. ✓
once				
long				
love				
began				
mum				
again				
every				
baby				
open				
gone				

Read–cover–write

Read each sentence and remember it. Then cover it and write it underneath.

I love to sing to the baby every day.

Mum has gone and left the door open again.

Answers

Page 4

1
pig	jam	lid
bus	zip	jab
gap	box	jet (or jot)

2
Mum and Dad   Hop on one leg.
a fishing net   The sun is hot.
not good: bad   Go to bed.
not thin: fat   Five and one makes six.
I can do it.   This is a cup.

Page 5

1
hand	and	ask
just	end	silk (or sink)
help	fast	sand
must	last	felt

2
from	black	plant
drop	still	grin
stop (or slop)	gran	flag
flop	step	stamp

Page 6

1
fish	much	think
rich	wish	ship
with	rush	flash
such	chop	thing

2
jar	corn	arm
car	dark	start
fork	bark	storm
star	sort	hard

Page 7

1
off	will	cross
miss	tell	duck
back	fizz	sniff

2
flock	stick	fill
neck	kiss	mess
puff	black	tick
fizz	fuss	doll

3 miss, well, pull, bell

Page 8

1. Two hands clap. two steps up the ladder
   fish and chips two ducks on the pond
   three jam jars Two plants grow in pots.
   lots of stars two flags

2. two frogs two desks
   two swings two stamps
   two bricks two drops
   two cards two socks

Page 10

1. zigzag visit
   sunset cobweb
   finish rabbit
   morning sandpit
   children seven

2. pecking, buzzing, barking, banging
   Dogs are <u>barking</u>. The hens are <u>pecking</u>.
   Bees are <u>buzzing</u>. She is <u>banging</u> the drum.

Page 11

1. ever, never, river, after, under

2. jumper letter
   silver finger
   sister supper
   number clever
   winter under

Page 12

1. boil join toy oil point
   boy joy spoil enjoy annoy
   coin soil coil foil toil

3. boiling joining pointing
   enjoying annoying spoiling

Page 13

1. day play pain gain train stay
   rain may say paint again away

2. snail, fail, nail, rail, tail (or tale)
   cake, make, take, bake, shake

3. game, came, same, name, flame, shame
   wave, gave, save, brave, cave, shave

Page 14

1
crossing the road
telling a joke
milking a cow
asking the time
missing the bus
fishing with a rod
jumping on the bed
starting (or stopping) the race
thinking with my brain
playing a game
sailing a boat

2
hanger	helper
buzzer	singer
sticker	player

Page 16

1
fly, dry, sky, try, cry
light, night, right, might, bright

2 *The words in brackets in each column might be given in a different order.*

ine	ive	ike	ide	ile	ight
nine	dive	like	side	smile	sight
line	drive	bike	slide	(mile)	(might)
(mine)	(five)	(Mike)	(tide)	(file)	(fight)
(fine)	(hive)	(hike)	(hide)	(tile)	(tight)

Page 17

1
beach → teach → reach
team → cream → dream
deep → weep → creep
keen → seen → been
heat → beat → seat
weed → speed → bleed

2
green	three
each	sleep
eat	sheep
tree	these

Page 18

1
snow	boast	show	grow	loaf
toast	slow	yellow	roast	blow

2 *The words in brackets might be given in a different order.*

oat	oad	oke	ose	ope	ole
boat	road	joke	nose	slope	stole
coat	toad	woke	rose	rope	(hole)
goat	load	smoke	(hose)	(hope)	(pole)
float		poke	(pose)	(pope)	

Page 19

1. cool, pool, fool, tool, stool, rule
   room, zoom, boom, broom, gloom, doom
   root, boot, toot, hoot, shoot, scoot
   noon, moon, soon, tune, spoon, June

2. The plane flew.
   The plants grew.
   The sky is blue.
   Give me a clue.
   Chew your food.
   Stick it with glue.
   We went to the zoo.

Page 20

1. bedroom   playtime   cornflakes (or cornflower/flour)
   farmyard   milkshake   teaspoon
   railway   sunshine   raincoat
   afternoon   laptop   bookshelf (or bookshop)

2. snowman   postcard
   seaside   Sunday
   sixteen   weekend
   nineteen   bluebell

Page 22

2. | ur | ir | er |
   |---|---|---|
   | burn | dirt | perch |
   | curl | girl | term |
   | turn | bird | |
   | surf | first | |
   | burst | skirt | |
   | hurt | third | |
   | church | shirt | |
   | | stir | |

Page 23

1. cow   crown
   now   town
   how   down
   wow   clown
   Pow!   frown

2. out, shout, about, spout, scout
   sound, found, round, ground, pound

3. howl   cloud   mouth   growl
   loud   proud (or prowl)   prowl (or proud)   south

Page 24

1. give, solve, sleeve
   have, above, leave
   live, glove, starve

2. page, large, rage
   stage, cage, age

3. bridge, fridge, budge, badge
   smudge, dodge, judge, nudge

Page 25

1. catch, sketch, match, witch (or watch), stitch, fetch, ditch, watch (or witch)

2.
teach	coach	torch	snatch
hutch	patch	church	perch
branch	bench	lunch	march
pinch	bunch	crunch	scratch
notch	pitch	arch	porch
latch	stretch	munch	beach

Page 26

1. 3 goats, 3 weeds, 3 matches
   3 teams, 3 patches, 3 coaches
   3 toys, 3 benches, 3 coins
   3 kisses, 3 nights, 3 snails
   3 girls, 3 wishes, 3 branches

2. A snake hisses. A boat floats.
   A teacher teaches. A can of pop fizzes.
   A plant grows. A rash itches.

Page 27

2. told, cold, sold, hold, bold, fold
   tall, call, wall, hall, ball, fall, small

Page 28

1. A rose has thorns. Blow the horn. north and south
   creep and crawl. a sleepy yawn. tall and short

3.
ore	aw	Other spelling
core	saw	door
score	paw	floor
more	draw	
before	straw	
shore	claw	

Page 29

1
good   foot
hood   flood
wool   blood

2
head   deaf
spread   tread
dead   instead

3 book, look, took, hook, shook

Page 30

2
w words   **wh words**
wind   where
went   when
with   why
wide   while
wish   which

3 whiskers, wheels

Page 31

1 knife, knee, know, knob, knew

3
Knock on the door.   Bend your knees.
Cut with a knife.   Knit me a scarf.
Kneel to pray.   Tie a knot.
Jack knows (or knew) the way.   a knight in armour

Page 32

1
pulled   barked   wished
sniffed   rushed   filled
joined   sailed   looked
turned   called   marched
crossed   toasted   stamped

2
On Monday, I missed the bus.
Last week, I helped Dad fix the car.
After a while, the kettle boiled.

Page 34

1
You hear with your ears.
year   beard
clear   Dear
near   tears

3 sneer, peer, cheer, beer, here

Page 35

1 chair, stair, hair, fair, pair
    dare, share, care, scare, stare
    bear, pear, wear, swear

2 Do pears grow on trees?   It's not here but there.
    Goldilocks met three bears.   Don't stare at me.
    I go up the stairs to bed.   I don't care.
    Brush my hair.   I wear a hat in winter.
    Sit on the chair.   three pairs of boots

Page 36

1 tick   pick   back   dark
    think   mark   bark   fork
    pack   bank   track   truck
    drink   rock   ask   thank

2 kit → kick → kid → kill
    skid → skip → skin → skill
    crab → crisp → crack → cross
    scar → scarf → scab → scare

Page 37

1 house   hiss   goose
    mouse   cheese   cross
    mess   horse   curse
    purse   dress   grease
    please   noise   pass

2 space, race, face, place, trace
    ice, dice, slice, nice, price
    chance, dance, glance, prance

Page 38

1 birthday party   The case is heavy.
    busy body   lime jelly
    hot and thirsty   silly billy
    nice and steady   copy cat
    Are you ready?   I feel happy.

2   monkey
    turkey   chimney   story
    fairy   donkey   honey

Published by Schofield & Sims Ltd,
7 Mariner Court, Wakefield, West Yorkshire WF4 3FL, UK
Tel 01484 607080

First published in 2013
Seventeenth impression 2025

© Schofield & Sims Ltd, 2013

Author: **Carol Matchett**
Carol Matchett has asserted her moral right under the Copyright, Designs and Patents Act, 1988, to be identified as the author of this work.

British Library Cataloguing in Publication Data
A catalogue record for this book is available from the British Library.
All rights reserved. No part of this publication may be reproduced, stored in a retrieval system, or transmitted in any form or by any means, electronic, mechanical, photocopying, recording or otherwise, without either the prior permission of the publisher or a licence permitting restricted copying in the United Kingdom issued by the Copyright Licensing Agency Ltd.

Commissioned by Carolyn Richardson Publishing Services

Design by Oxford Designers & Illustrators
Printed in the UK by Page Bros (Norwich) Ltd

ISBN 978 07217 1212 3

Schofield & Sims

the long-established educational publisher specialising in maths, English and science

Learn to spell in three simple steps
Remember • Try it • Read–cover–write

Accurate spelling improves fluency in writing and is vital to clear communication. **Schofield & Sims Spelling** is a structured and rigorous programme designed for Key Stages 1 and 2 – but also suitable for some older students. At the heart of the programme is a set of six pupil books, accessible to all who have a basic understanding of letter–sound relationships. Correct answers are provided at the back of each book so that pupils may mark their own work.

Ideal for both whole-school and independent learning, this comprehensive and high-quality series builds on pupils' phonic knowledge while also helping them to understand how word structure and meaning can help them to spell words. Providing excellent preparation for the national tests, the **Schofield & Sims Spelling** activities:

- systematically introduce spelling conventions – and revise those already taught
- explore word structure and the relationship between words of shared origin
- suggest strategies for remembering common 'exception words' (also known as 'tricky words')
- teach pupils how to monitor and correct their own spelling
- encourage them to write sentences from memory or dictation.

As pupils work through each book, the intensive practice provided will enable them continually to develop, consolidate and improve their skills, encouraging them towards effective spelling for life.

Areas covered by **Spelling 1** include:

- segmenting words into phonemes and selecting from alternative spellings
- using spelling rules for adding **s** and **es**
- adding suffixes **ing**, **ed** and **er**, where no change is needed to the root word
- dividing words into syllables
- applying spelling guidelines (for example, **ck**, **tch**, **ve**, **dge** at the end of words).

Also available: a **Teacher's Guide**, providing detailed teaching notes that suggest how best to explain and explore each learning point, a **Teacher's Resource Book**, containing copymasters that support teaching, assessment and record-keeping, and **free downloads for teachers**, available from the Schofield & Sims website.

The complete range of books is as follows:

Spelling 1	(Key Stage 1)	ISBN 978 07217 1212 3	**Spelling 4**	(Key Stage 2)	ISBN 978 07217 1215 4
Spelling 2	(Key Stage 1)	ISBN 978 07217 1213 0	**Spelling 5**	(Key Stage 2)	ISBN 978 07217 1216 1
Spelling 3	(Key Stage 2)	ISBN 978 07217 1214 7	**Spelling 6**	(Key Stage 2)	ISBN 978 07217 1217 8
Spelling Teacher's Guide		ISBN 978 07217 1218 5	**Spelling Teacher's Resource Book**		ISBN 978 07217 1219 2

ISBN 978-07217-1212-3

FSC MIX Paper | Supporting responsible forestry FSC® C023114

ISBN 978 07217 1212 3
Key Stages 1 & 2
Age range 5–12 years
£4.95
(Retail price)

For further information and to place your order visit
www.schofieldandsims.co.uk or telephone 01484 607080